THE
Music Laid her SONGS
IN LANGUAGE

Other books by the author:

THE
Music Laid her SONGS
IN LANGUAGE

MICHAEL HASLAM

PUBLICATIONS
2001

Published by Arc Publications
Nanholme Mill, Shaw Wood Road
Todmorden, Lancs. U.K. OL14 6DA

Design by Tony Ward
Printed at the Arc & Throstle Press
Nanholme Mill, Todmorden, Lancs.

ISBN 1 900072 68 8

Acknowledgements:
to "infernal methods" for delightful
pastime oral call response (green
withen aura) which appeared in
april eye poems for peter riley

The Publishers acknowledge financial
assistance from Yorkshire Arts Board

CONTENTS

GREEN WITHEN AURA

(Delightful Pastime Oral Call Response.
For Peter Riley)

I had been following, or so I felt, a futile so-called
calling, and a false trail, and I had failed.
Footloose I lay, and heard another sweet cascade
of little falls, and something solitary, smaller:
the green withens aura.

There's an air to the wild upland willows.
                Halo To The Sallows. Hello There
young green yellow willow warbler
footles through light leafs
an odd fluff-suited, coloured, call. Subtle
the way it's fluted this june.
    An air of blue
veils the face of the day-time moon.
The young out of a bog-edge nest are flown.
    An air you feel
is like benevolence, if you could only cage it
like a lark in pastoral romance.
    A waving air:
a one-year wand of one fond fairy
    salix-frond, forms out of somnolence
in woodland dress.

And, in co-incidence, another air, another day
    on folly field I almost heard
the butterly marine band play
    with the shine blown away
with the fairies in the shale.

THE
Music Laid her SONGS
IN LANGUAGE

Music Laid Her Egg in Language.
Ovum of a bird.
                    The word *Idea*
– an ideal bird, an ideal local place, just as it is –
is generally mental in its adjectival form.
The richly-coloured feathers that we find in fact
have been attached at some points in the past
to reproductive acts. The flurry pairs
with after sex, to nest, insects and sticks.

The image *Wish* is asymmetrical in that
it only goes the same way as the stars: no wish
to change the past has ever hatched.
A bad clutch of regrets collapse.
I personally make my own repairs. The cluster sticks.

Try this one: I is as the Figure I, a stick
in clay agglomerates, in mud and other matter
after flood in sludge. The water
of a sudden was dislodged. A gush of bubbles
but the cluster wouldn't budge. The one mistake
I made was, plant my stake in hope
        that it might fledge.

                    *

I woke with what bird-angel I had fought with
forked prong, a smitten hammer, fiery pair
        of tongues. This tang
to have refined to tine. Bird-angel thought had told me
I had wrought her sculpture wrong. And much
        as I resist the touch of shame I must admit
I have a rope encased in strangulated song.

                    *

The Figure One is watching
something ancient in the shape of heavy traffic
through the clearing of the nymphs. The figure smirks
    and thinks to call them
academic lasses Sapphic. They are hard at work –

cleaning, washing, changing bandages. His gaze is
on the gauze and flock of cotton catching hairs,
and what he hears is *This is Mystic*, this is that
stripped off the wound. He sees his quirk
sat on the mound enjoying favours like he were their
    eunuch of the month. That little
tongue-twister is sickening. His breathing
quickly thickens. Breeding, bleeding, nymphs and months
don't rhyme. And Music still refuses to Personify.

      The Figure I
can not identify
the brush-head with his stick.
The figure I saw music changing sex.

      As if I could
be pacified.
The figure came unstuck from what I saw
in shaw lee wood.

      *

It is a Sunday in the given rhythm, and there's nothing
urgent I can think of. The agenda has been satisfied. I'm in
no hurry for another story of the flurry of the birds over the
waterfall, nor a drama on the wet and dreadful moor, or any
other places where a figure met a force. I'm here to make
a verbal sketch of oaken shaw wood hall, a fairly pure
objective. The door is opening for light refreshments, sticky
sweetmeats, pop and teas. I can please myself with leaflets
for amusement. Wooden banks, a knotty bench, the local
history of formal settlements expressed; in ingle nook a
wooden form; old settle in the hall. The muse is in
her olden days today, and most sedate, at home in the
museum. Families approve each other. All are well-behaved.
There is nothing here to violently shake the rattle of my fancy
I'm an artist, and am glad of that.

Out in the garden haze and grace elide
with blooms across the park they used to graze.
Across the yard there stands a shed filled with
old obsolete machines. Only the very mildest breeze,
I'm feeling only very gently metaphoric, and no urgency
as far as I can see disturbs the dustbins in this scene.
It could be *This is Peace* it maybe means.

In just this lapse, a sort of slack, I heard the slipping
of a thumbsneck latch. I watched a woman use an almost hidden
door to leave. She looks to me just as I imagine Psyche
understanding what eye-contact means, I wish I knew –
I wish to know. She wears a skirt and has car keys.
She disappears between the trees. She looked to me I'm glad to say
as if I please.
I think to sing, so this is just a light
hearth-passage entry catch. *House Body Dream Airs Ease.*

*

A warbler all fluffed up with instant plumage
breathes.
  The natural accounts of courting I suppose
apply.
  How can you keep your clutch of mental eggs
undamaged and alive?
  Do you beware. Another magpie. Not all messages
are meant for you.
  A kestrel
waving like a paper up on high cold edge
between the wakes of wind-distressed trees.
  Are meant for me. No omen
but I couldn't manage. That is true.

.

*

Gag. Gauge. How to engage with Language
  again at my age, and each year more
the curdle of the moorland curlew over keelham gate;
a tally-score of weekends on the beer.
  I favour simple rhetoric for walking in the dignity
of merely being here. I could occlude
  a sky too loud, an oracle, a cry, a call:
ill may it ail you, cooed or crowed, but chilling cold.
  No superstition, but the setting in a certain light
of literary fear.
  The sky too quiet now and clear as failure.

*

The squawk of an hysteric brunt
        both cock and hen hath borne has sent
curt notes of sharp distinguishable anguish:
blighted troth; the plight of marriage; music
for the costume dramas of another age.
        A trope of spirit slipped out of the door
and sang above the stammer. No I couldn't
think of something so becoming –

I the jaded figure with his rotted copper sulphate plumbing
dumped in a muktub skip. Recycle if beyond repair.
A rusted bedstead in the reed mud sump up on the tip
at little moor. No nearer to the curse's source.

There is a cock as laid an egg.

That is a frigging lie.
There was a horrid treading in the forest shed.
Impulsive threads lie deadened.

                *

Music came up to the ears and filled
        a water bucket full of flowers for the funeral.
She took two steps into the wind
        and all her hair flew out in strings
over the verge of tears.

                *

A flight of moths, flitting the rigging
                feast on forest mast.
The uninvited ghost come through
        the webbing of the attercobs.
Behind the windowseat I found a colony of the
colopterous woodworming beetles. Rid the nest house self
of boring, stifling, unearthing nothing personal in suffering
the tedium in suffocating airlessness inside alive.

Forty years ago one day
a chalk-tip splintered, and an enigmatic scrap of maths
was wiped clean off the board. This triggered off
a fit of giggles. Figure-brain finds something funny
in the algebraic squiggles that it doesn't understand.
So I was stood out in a corridor. His giggling wouldn't stop.
And there I was perfectly careless.

A handle to the attic light
I couldn't grasp her metaphor.
A lock released a curl of hair, a door
        but opened on a flight at vespers
and an air of giddy bats. Alas.

                *

The Figure I again stand here and sees
        the river run uphill and disappear
into a bush of blips of light
around a molten mountain sun –
                        a river budding
out at spindly wells, and mouthing
        rushbed issues. I can imagine
what the figure must have felt to find
the one thing that they called the source
abstracted rose in an adulterated landfill.

                *

Geology, I told myself again, is plain
and stands for nothing. Bedrock sandstone grains
of sand. The riffles of a drift. *You mean to say*
that Music never laid her pebble in among
the layers of erogenous geology? What's this
quartz pebble pearl? Something for Nothing?
Music, stripped of all associates, stood solid
to that mouthing-cum-delirium of his.

*

If music lays her eggs in language language must be
nest and all around it. The squamose squab lay
on the slab. That is traditional language poetry. Never
quite at its best. And all my fledgling hopefuls may
reveal a hint of something squalid. Nothing pure
as water touching on the bottom in the sand. The blows
of life come on in waves of hot and cold.
    We squat. We make a dump. The wind blows on.

*

An embryo reptilian looks in the sky
So this is how I scry a stolen mirror shine.
    Vermillion on soft black colour slime.
The strings and globs of come and gone.
There spread a gossamer along
I do not want to say the thighs
of heather moorland but I have done.

*

I never reined or bit a horse
free play but just
the upshot of small fricative excitements.
Locally the gum goes blue. Find me
a deep depression, I'll stop letting go.

*

I have also gone to great lengths to try to ensure that
unities of time and place in any verse, if not obeyed
have been at least askance observed. What season is it
now? Don't tell me autumn.

Along the cold coast I had cast my coat
across her breast and shoulders. It is like
a freak or shawl of snow. I placed my cold hand
in the shiverings of sibilance. Ey, Love,
is there a bubble in the bosom of thy silence? –
That is just too sad. I found some snake eggs once
but now I can't remember when. Hold an aversion
to the earth at arm's length. Music made
herself sound ovoid. What I find ingenious
is quite ideal in progeny and gender.
Sometimes there is just an overwhelming urge to cry,
like when I have my cornet twisted in a tantrum.

How tender white and abstract music dawns
on us at thorny hippens: wind and strings,
dark light and livid. All the other verdure equally
as vivid. Ash buds turn magenta/virid.
And especially the maytree once again looks fit to blanch.
It is in one's nature to repeat oneself, I had asserted,
sounding solemn.

*

The quirk of wit that let us fancy even now
poetic scientists are teasing out is somewhere likened
to a mischief in the branches of a family tree.
It was awakened by mistake in a dream:
a hope to pair among the tumblers off the canopy
and be one with the vigorous thermal airs. O O
Ovarians! O Geneology!

Not to be analytical, one even thought the quirk
could be behind the rash of allergy. In hebden bridge
they're not so much poetic as inclined
to gorgeous therapy. Down in the mill I used to work
how one hysteric shriek can hold you in its long
hypnotic span. A matter of compression fitting,
so I come at it, a spanner in each hand.

A denser dale mentality – what is the point? –
relieved by chance a dazzle of trough-water bubbles –
not so much a metaphor as an ideal of dance.

*

On down by the river there's a figure
in a basket laid her eggs. The river forks.
Long stoney spit. A sort of strand. There's my familiar.

Abrupt shift up the cliff to scan
she laid herself in the green withens
under black stone edge. What of
the fluster of the warblers in the sedge,
the theft of favours, and a shameless flirting
of the feathers in a briar? It is covered.

*

Laid on a length by way of hill head edge
and down some glum and sodden soakaway
by mosses to the bland extreme of dribbling sands
and streetlight strings, the strands again and
     promenades along the coast. I shall forgive you
on the littoral of old vergivia. There Music spread
her trestle-table legs. We mashed her juices
in a vat pastiche. Here's One
from PolyOlbion: Here's to
the Egg-Pie Lasses in the spirit of the lust they bear for
Bag-and-Hornpipe Lads. Here's the three
mersey nymphs we know as flixton partington and cadishead.
The undines swim the long canal in pollutant solution.
I would there were a wishing well at irlam.
Is the coaling basin gone? We must protest
at what provides us with no work. Her scream was heard
in all the nooks of the palatinate. We look again
for some improvement in the patient state of water.
How she felt the liner bearing in across the moss.
Say no to rape.
Here's to the odour of old warrington.
Here's to the water lust and drink to change
the shape again. For irony to work
she's too far gone.

*

hey ho hollidaye and on
with the white cider shepherds of the park end scrub,
the soaked, the scared, the sacred and the sad,
the old, the cold, the henpecked and the generally scolded
mostly men,
    the droner too-predictable, the mad, the bad –
the best and worst minds of no generation have been
    literally had.

        *

Anywhere
the sound of pipe's repeated spatter
on the stone again. The drift from solid
all-in-one location, into heaven, physical relief
again. The golden piping of a plover in among
a lapwing flock again. Out to the oystercatcher's lucid flutes
come over you all shivery again. Again
her shifted-from-the-shoulder shawl, again.
The shadow follows wings of The Ovarians
    above the passage in a cross the bar again.

Nowhere nothing
neither urgent nor superfluous again. A range
from bridge and terrace, the arcade of stars,
to settle for a conscious cup with handsome wings,
a charm, the bobbin with a string long snapped,
a goose's neb amid the flocking host,
    the fledgling worm, a new romance,
the ruby light-display that's even
             in the sun-bank hidden
when the flies at dusk come in
with swallows to the midden where the midges
dance again.

        *

I hear she mews through mistal walls.
Telephone calls.
A cluster.
Notes on drama, dream and trauma.

A note of all souls. Who heard hullet cote owls
    where dark and stoney lanes meet in a fork.
What got my throat was a summer note about the cat-
with-a-swallow-in-her-teeth duet.
        One awful time we used to hear
the calving screams of Belgian Blues, night after night
bray from the brand-new laithe at stoney royd.
        A Note.
I have these sirens muffled inwardly.
Old News.
I much prefer the stretch to hearing
        of a far-off river.
I am less annoyed. A note:
Find out about the phantom sibling, how it found
the space inside a self-reflexive soul.
Unfortunately
it was found uncomfortably snuffled.
Me,
I see my lights are on but I am not at home.

*

We are up some siding from
        the tracks of *music laid her* language songs.
A sketch. Describe
the boiler-slag and other cinder tippings
as a bank of levelled heaps:
                        a gabled valley-crest
of back-to-backs. Make it look
quite picturesque. A new romantic vista
of the valley death. And not
untruthful. Dirty
pastel mist of idle waste
in some confusion mixed with astley brook
and run on down to coke choked breath.
I have the art to use how light dark echoes
        with the still sound shadows
and a local calling
Have you seen our smutty beauty hereabouts?

Over the footbridge down at waters meetings.
Loud colliding. Glassinesses in the cinder. Ruby
in the light reflex. The lines in some perspective find
the water-treatment works.

I have willed you here to lull you lob.
You are only playing with words.
You know what rhymes with them.
Emerging empty as lugubrious more mournful
in the gravel where the plot was laid you lost
your marbles in the middle of that slaggy puddle.
You can see what rhymes with dream and drama
written in reflections of the sky above
your armature in love.

                        *

You would think that with a pair of tongs
we could get a grip on this slippery ground:
the shadow of some trees down steep clough hole.
You would think we could run with the sun concurrence
and attain transparence. Bugger rot, what was the point
of a spirit spot? I shouldn't wonder but you love
long sylvan drops, and feel immune from drippings
from the eaves into the fool's own zone of song:

> Like Plop and Cuff
> how you do tease
> me soul went blue
> the black pool wakes
> and if it please
> you never leave off pleasure
> if however poor your treasure
> you can never touch with irony
> but to return each after fire
> every blossoming of trees.

*

Up at the trickle well I didn't wish but felt
     a pretty penny drop in my economy. Plain water
makes a poor but honest cleaning fluid. We have suffered
     much at work from frightful volatiles. I'd rather
brew a bland emulsion for a water-spirit glue.

Life is hard and quite aesopified my morals.
Sour grape fox, and, fox again, the one stuck in
the cistern of the rivulets, who sang out to the goat up
     on the rim about how sweet the water is,
my favourites. I want to ride up on a reader's back.

It is a balm to be laid off. What will you do
when *music laid her* songs is done? I'll take my brush
(the fox again) in sunshine and in shade and sweep
the passages for two quiet weeks in the shed alone
instead of pay in lieu. I sweep a tidy heap
of swarf and now and then
     I only want a shovel for the bin. I can
demand no credit. I have understood that none is due.
I'd like to write. *I'll weep* and stuff. I would
          if it were true. Come drink. O be a man.

There is a low, low valley spot, so angled that
a winter sun has never lit, a black damp cleft
deep slit ravine, a twisted neck of woods between
the steeps and eaves, deep underbanks,
                              bare dripping trees –
A cold spot down the neck
awoke the quirk.
Just knock it on the head.

The hoofs of thunder either were the weather
of the further mother-valley stations being shaken
        by the passage of a long coal train.
Another change of music lay delayed.
Quirk up again. Awake.

By brigg head well, bog eggs,
the music strayed up over round along a long
catchwater drain and down
by goyt syke sough. Some places
in the *music laid her* songs do not exist.
Ah whisht, ah whisht, but what were wished
        were but a whitish hiss.
The other roughness is a far-off river.

From daubhill brick to midgley grit,
from were to where almost as fayre
were fur. An air. From longworth eagley
bradshaw tong to colden, hebden, calder
where he lingers as an older figure
with his stick, whereat I languished, but

music relayed.
I stick so long I aged. That's it.

NOTES ON *Music*

i. Spots

There's a spot in the brain where blitz-streaks crack;
where lightning strikes, and twin squibs hatch;
whence lace in twine unspools as fast
    as stars' expanse
through helices of spring's abstraction
to an in-ward vacant sea.

It rains on an adjacent spot of ruined dwellings
which the spirits of a past advance frequent,
forgotten spots, the muse-band at low frequency.

Spirits? I can think of as if I were one among them
watching a cold-front clouding high flat ridge
    and sending fingers over flagstone edge –
the illusion closed with the last high sunshaft
obliterated in aesthetic dissolution. Hearken too
an owl over the effluent guffaw of land-drains,
and the darkened tones of the overflow. It must be time
that takes us whole with both the silences and all
our belches, all our laughs. Spirits! I am enthused,
    are a special privilege of the daft.

*

There's a spot of sharp forks in the stars
and moonshine on the bilious nimbus
and the outline of the flats. It looks
like one of those ghost places
where the psyche wakes:
on the track up rake head to the pike, Hah!
I have stood like a lad, a stone along the heights.

*

Morning rush-hour, down a pokey hole, I own
I missed my turn completely, sat so long
at bridge gate lights the red again came round.
    Turn thoughts from exercising in a cinder ginnel
through the green love affair down spinney dell,
and little fear, the colour of my shirt's unsuitable,
upon the whole, and all the while I hear the horns
like hoofbeats of a forlorn hope. When at last
I am got in gear, I know they are bound
to be calling me stupid, a hog for the queue behind.
I think I might try to describe
    the seeing of blank verse in colour.

*

Forget the spots, and do the mazy riddle
of the marbles to a grid set in the middle.
Drink and may music lay
her pebbles on the cover of your drain.

One spot when psyche's twin was woken
to a blinking landing light. There was a man
was drawn to bars to obviate
the flashes in gibberish. Drink here

We welcome spinners ever drawing lines
out of the flocculence.
Can you put this lad up with a serious flock
of socially heretical crackle?
Democracy. A comic opera. Soap
with a stain in the middle.

Twite pipe and thus
     the thrust of pipit twitter.
Thus the black sharp specks, a starling flock split
     reunite.
The giddy wren does genuinely spin
     the conjugals in holes.
A wagtail pair
the colour of a young sun shed
on sudden showers through unclouded holes
repair and there
the stream ribbons through stepping stones.

*

ii. The Frightful Cook

The frightful cook spikes with a fork
the pepper he sliced through the heart
by knife;
    with jilted shoulder-spasms
addresses air with sweeping jealous whoppers
of a spatula.

The spirit that supports him in these lies
    as his familiar black skillet spits
hot lipid drops over the cooker's edge
to maculate in spots the ground linoleum.

On black edge he has used to crack his eggs
and sticky spots unswallowed of a horror.
    Once-too-oft reheated, this soft rice he forks
but inexplicably upsets the skillet and retreats
to solitary wine believing thirst
    will not desert him

*

iii. Desert Song

The little cock looks like a dunnock
    at the cuckoo's nest.
Something is wrong. And someone sings
a wild song of the waste of heart's deserts.
A cock as laid an egg. It looks
more like a cockatrice to me that thing.

        *

iv. Glum Hanging Falls

Once one blue damselfly the colour of
    a nylon rope was unmistaken by a swallow
taking loops through trees out over falling water.

The shock, a joke to choke on: yoked: unyoked:
it jerks the spine and gives the jaw a jolted grin.
It leaves you idling badly in a dawdling spin.
It might have left you a yard of yarn, a broken shed,
    a creel to play in.
It will learn you. And it ended then.

*

v. An Ash A She

A windless blue november day, a young ash tree
without a breath, without a breeze,
shed all of her last leaves, and shook
the tresses of her keys.

Dry air, dry shower, as a fall of hair.
A lisp, as leaves' fine echo of their landing
on the cinder gravel. And the fall was slow.
And stripped she looked regretfully deciduous to me.

What is she like? She's not unlike
bright fay who has her physical electric patch.
On touch the static splinters into fractions.
She had me so elated but
her cold lips parting checked my peak.

*

vi. The Spirit Versed

When first I met the barguest thirst
on withens gate in the abysmal rain
wrapped in my sodden shawl:
me and the boggart, we exchanged directions
to the snowy woods, and to a hidden gabled hall,
and a thirst for a thaw.

Sketches brushed with flakes of ice.
Brushed off, the vision of the snow.
Uncoiling strings of icy winter hail.
The shape thirst shifts.

A calling wail winds over noah dale.
I cannot think
the spirit Love, the spirit Thirst, both all at once
to some avail until the april fields arise
with matings more audible;
And I can get off in spring wood hollow
on the sounding falls.
A no-sound vision rushes off:
The surprising flight of an owl.

*

vii. A Lake Below High Brow

There runs a sike across the english waste
to feed her goit. You know the billy house goit
that lodges water by the mill head shed?
I could show you how. It took a millyard years
to reach this half-obliterated-by-the-shadow space.

In still psychology, she feeds her goat
on willow-leaves. Still state: psyche umbellifer
of a ghostly elder, moonlit, shows her flower face.

Pure moonshine coats a pool of coloured oils.
The dilapidation is becoming undespoiled.
The millyard shadows shed,
        and mica flakes star cobble. Lunar quick,
a little slick from a deep ceramic sink.
        Same moonsheen
off the sagging roof-flags of a long-ago-
        co-opted laithe. The water gurgles. Races.

First light and the millyard birds'll quirk.
The laughing fool turns giddy at the piss-take.
Comic effects. That was my mistake.
A shelduck drake re-echoes mockery off damside rocks.
I'll enjoy the ducks, being a quack myself.
But listen, I'm serious about this, it doesn't have to rhyme
        and a reservoir is a lake.

Give us a break.

SECOND DRAUGHT-SHAPED MOVEMENT OF NOTES

Fallen over, and half-off a sofa
while the white detergent bubbles round the plates
steeped in the sink pop out of sight, excited
by a dripping tap

hold the breath, and redraw a draught,
     throat rhythmic snore
held in a vast abeyance, flows
     like seaweed in a salt dream:

Grey Groynes, and greenly sea-mossed
     ferrous piles and stakes
and perilous defiles of rock.
A place to wet your bottom on the water in the sand.
To depilate the sealace and to pop the bladder wrack

and suitable as much for solace as for lack:
the very place you find you lost
     the fundamental plot, but look
at where you're sat. Come let us go
and watch the river snakes
give osculum a great waste of oceanic calm.

Just then as you'd expect this
awkward gull walks up. That squark
should wake him to a supper cup.
Slips supplicated.

                    *

FOUR BALLADIC IDYLLS

A young wet sun was spreading beams
on spring bank green wood shelters
and the stone booth royd and ing schole field,
    and shone on shields and sheddings, over shelf
and wood shaw dene bank dwellings.

May was late but when she came
with rushes like a beauty queen
    from budding to her petals cream in green
and then again with rushes
    shows a flagrant thorny cladding
from a bonnet with a rush to be berried.

The rushes made a fan for the marsh
but also gave them fairies in the mouth.
The rushes of the lads I mean.
They could have sworn with joy and wonder
at the rush bed fan of nan hole clough,
and at her schole and dwelling under
hawthorn skirts in a ring of the hippens.

How did I get here? Back to when
up slack house lane by striding gate
were come this throng of young
gay birkenshaw with bracken fernyhough
and long bob hollin rake of little worth
and thistlethwaite that spits i'th'trough
and crabtree bent with creeping twitch
all itch to make a crazy beeline
keen as whippets in a sticky patch of rough
for pollard sticks.

This was the gang, and they were come
to mingle in among a gaggle of them
    siren lasses filling jugs up
at the treacle-well, where trickle drops
colloquially dally in idyllic nooks.

The lads rise to their knees, in sporting scenes:
one lad shy in the shield of the school
with one eye for the issue in the hair-grass
    fringed with sorrel, rumex, and a tongue to taste
the acetosa, sweet as lemon drops;
    another licking lips
who dares to name the prominence a labia;

and not the first a shining birk that stands
with roots curled over sill lip whose reflected silvers
slip and wet spot marks the rocks as water falls,
but the wicken slim that parks a thrush up withens rough
the moment when the golden pipes amid a field of green
    and twisting plovers
over pipit twite and uprush of the common lark
and all that may but hark at him and his
so wick a trunk and thrust:

A shriek arose up from the stubbing bottom
of a rocky spot of rape and river capture,
    mingled, pinned
in furzen shanks from which
    the shriek arose and ran:
a blood-wraith from the waste down
shaw wood tip and up rush candle clough
and over red mires flat and on
the stoney cairn of high knoll edge it sang.

For a lad in the reflection of electric lamps
in black glass of a bus held at the angle
of a junction by the lights,
      the coal damp mist and drizzle hung
on river bottoms and the long tong moor.
There's an intensity in knowing where you are.

And when the last steam whistle blew at halt
before the tunnel beyond entwistle
      a funnel chuffed on entry under
bradshaw, grey stones, broad head height.
      And how it falls on astley bank, the cinder levels,
and the playing fields of sharples park.
      And how it sounds and lights
the mills of longworth in the night.
And how the dunscar tongue at the extended borough terminus
      begins to turn the brook to burn
the coal seams just to heat and spoil the water
all for nothing in the long run when it doesn't matter
what the plot but hark and look and learn.

It learned me what. Say how to grasp
      a sprig of hips. As if in some reflection
I had wished for this
      balladic idyll come to black stone ruin
through the gossamer on pollenating heath
with all the aimlessness of willowherbal fluff:

Totting up on the fingers there's a balance:
nothing under black knoll edge but greaves
of withins and a stream of hate for love
but to his credit there's a love of haws and of
quick-shooting wicken, shed of iris
      in a delph of yellow flag, the eclogues
of the pace-egg recobbled, broken glass
      and mill-dam flashes under stoodley wood.

A music song so long and aged as this is bound
to sag sometimes. The last leaves of a pallid elder
weighted down by, by the bright umbellifer
so berried. I've been adding sugar
to the colour of the wine. There spreads
a florid fungus on the floor of rotten wood.
    I have felt sad
to see the bright spots of a virus fit to shed.
I came the long way down and sunk
a roof of sandstone slate to find
solace so late, at the end of the day, when the truth shines out
that it's all over bar the sheep at moor end gate.

It's as if I'd been given a wish but when I gazed
at the godmother beauty the giver
I had been so dazed and looked so deep
    I must have wished for nought
but listened:

There's a fox,
and there's an overflow I call
a goit-sluice to the river;

there's a spirit passes like a shadow
without weight that slips
across the back to breed
    and dissipate
enjoyments of the waste.

The *butterly marine band*, estheria, reticuloceras, is found in shales between strata of kinderscout grit. One grit-band up from kinderscout, and we're into what is know in calderdale as scotland flag. Above scotland flag, under the crow-hill crown of midgley moor, and we're on midgley grit, set in which lies *folly field:* a squarish patch of grass, now inclined to bent, bounded by broken walls, as an exception to the heather moor: a place, I was told, of whitsun fairs, before my days – stalls; flapping canvas; a brass band.

The *adjectival form of the noun* Idea, is of course the word *Ideal*, which sets up on its own the enterprise of thought as interplay among assorted nouns. My own bias of thought is more Gregory Bateson than Jacques Lacan, and more William Shakespeare than Sigmund Freud. The *academic lasses Sapphic* sounded like sirens to a laddish reserve, but the crisis passed.

The *oakenshaw wood hall* is nearly purely fictional, but has survived poor rates, community charge, and council tax, as the pride of a local authority. The gentleman who built it would have been circumspect between parties, but cromwellian in his own biblical independence.

Hebden bridge, in my cosmology (experience), stands for a certain locus of human exchange and emotion; an object of love and despair; a melting pot tone; and a town of social resources.

Michael Drayton's *Poly-Olbion* (1612-22) is a work I much enjoy, but doubt to recommend. Every nymph, you should know, has a river. Their collective echoes rebound from the deaf wall of *blackstonedge.* They fill the vales of mersey. Although you may find a clay pipe works spoil tip hard by the springs of irwell, and the slack of sharney ford, as a concerned reader you should know that long before the great steam despoliation, the name of bacup was *foul beck hope*, suggesting to me that peaty liquid acids, running through raw iron and coal, effused an aura only doubtfully potable. Drayton's thirty songs, a great work of arcadian pedantry was born as out-of-date as my own more humble and constricted efforts in the similar veins of desire.

In *hey ho hollidaye* (a refrain from avgvst, aegloga octaua of the shepheardes calender) I slander certain *white-cider shepherds*, who, in truth, frequent no *park end scrub*, but provide a civil meeting-point in a sedate coign of the memorial gardens, close by the (elysian fields of) calder holmes. On awaydays they may enjoy the architectural halifax piece hall. In my poem they might sit for the eternal object of puritan legislation.

Researchers into the field of *treacle wells* might look no further than the headwaters of blackburn's darwen, see the nymph and thrill with glee.

Lancashire and yorkshire really hold the waste land of the pennines as a place name like in popple's common. *Daubhill* rhymes with cobble, but the daub we guess was baked in famous *brick*. The tykes made mullions from *midgley grit*. By *goit sike sough*, how much the water suffered only hurt the pains of love.

The *Notes* go over all this ground again, including a haunting strange lightning-struck sea-coast, which was where beauty originally laid her eggs. The mock-triumph of *balladic idylls* makes for a farcical vindication of a life's project: to let the whole weary band of poetic image settle easily on an equally worn topography, so that lumb falls, for instance, exactly where it stands, and thence would feed (again by goit) a spirit founding arcadia among remains and ruins, textile mills down deep ravines. The transcendent universals rolling over rocky bowls are presently exhorting us to play because we're back at work tomorrow. So:

> Up up my friend and quit but stop
> the day is fine the snow is white
> the air is blue and bright, but wait:
> the paths are closed for an alert of foot and mouth.

M.H. Sun march fourth o-one

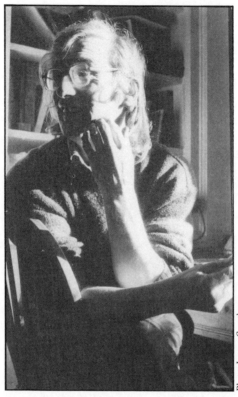

Photo: Joanne Crowther

MICHAEL HASLAM was born in Bolton, Lancashire in 1947, and has lived near Hebden Bridge, Yorkshire since 1970. Widely published in the network associated with 'The Cambridge School of Poetry', he founded the small press *Open Township*, and edited the magazine *folded sheets* (1985-91). In 1995 Carcanet Press published his collected poems *A Whole Bauble*. He has worked as a labourer most of his life, and is currently a machine-operator milling and drilling in Mytholmroyd.